To all the imaginative young artists out there, may this book be your canvas for boundless creativity and joyous exploration. Let your imagination soar as you fill these pages with vibrant colors and magical scenes. Remember, there are no mistakes in art, only beautiful surprises waiting to be discovered. Happy coloring!"

Bruno Caldevilla
2024

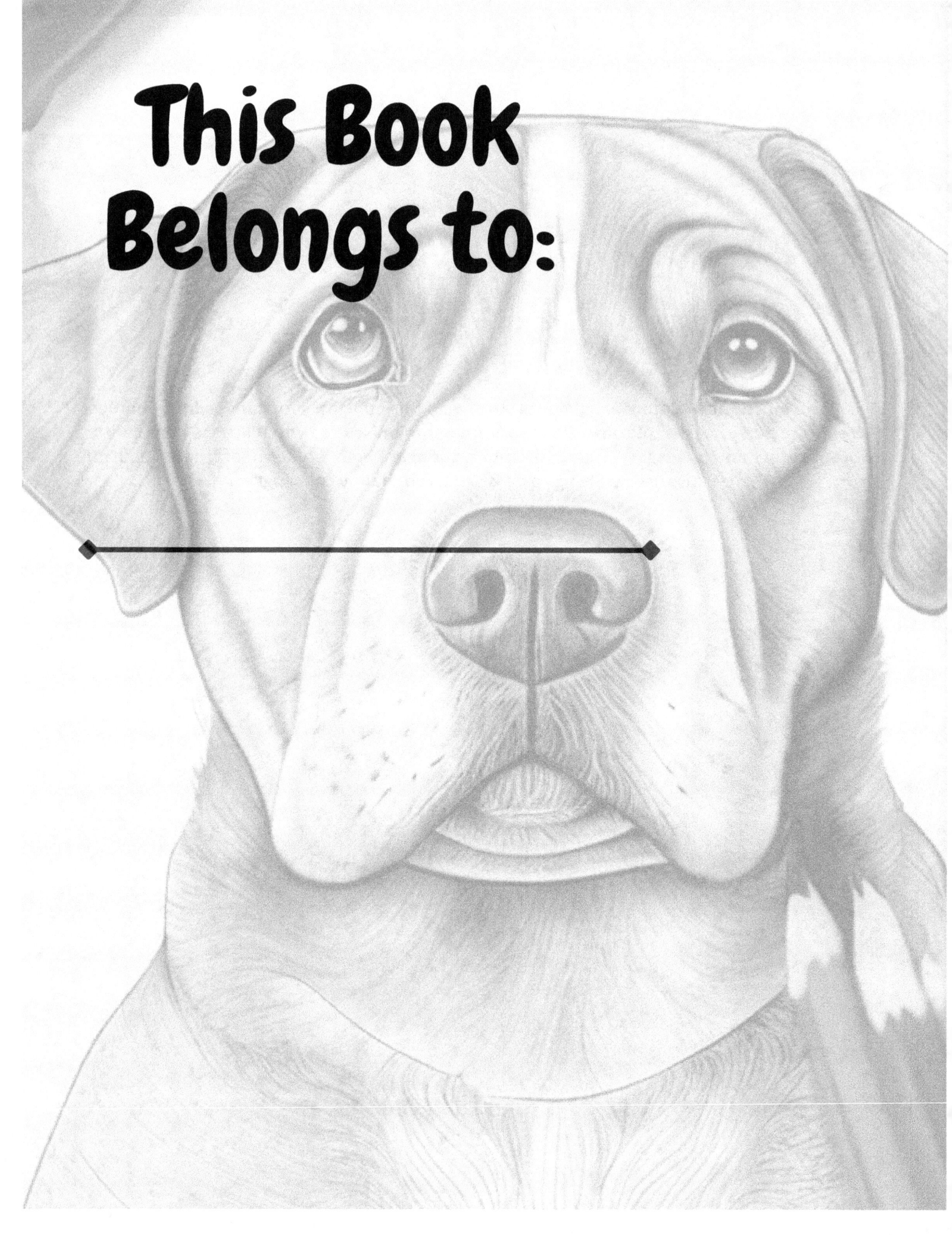

Test color page

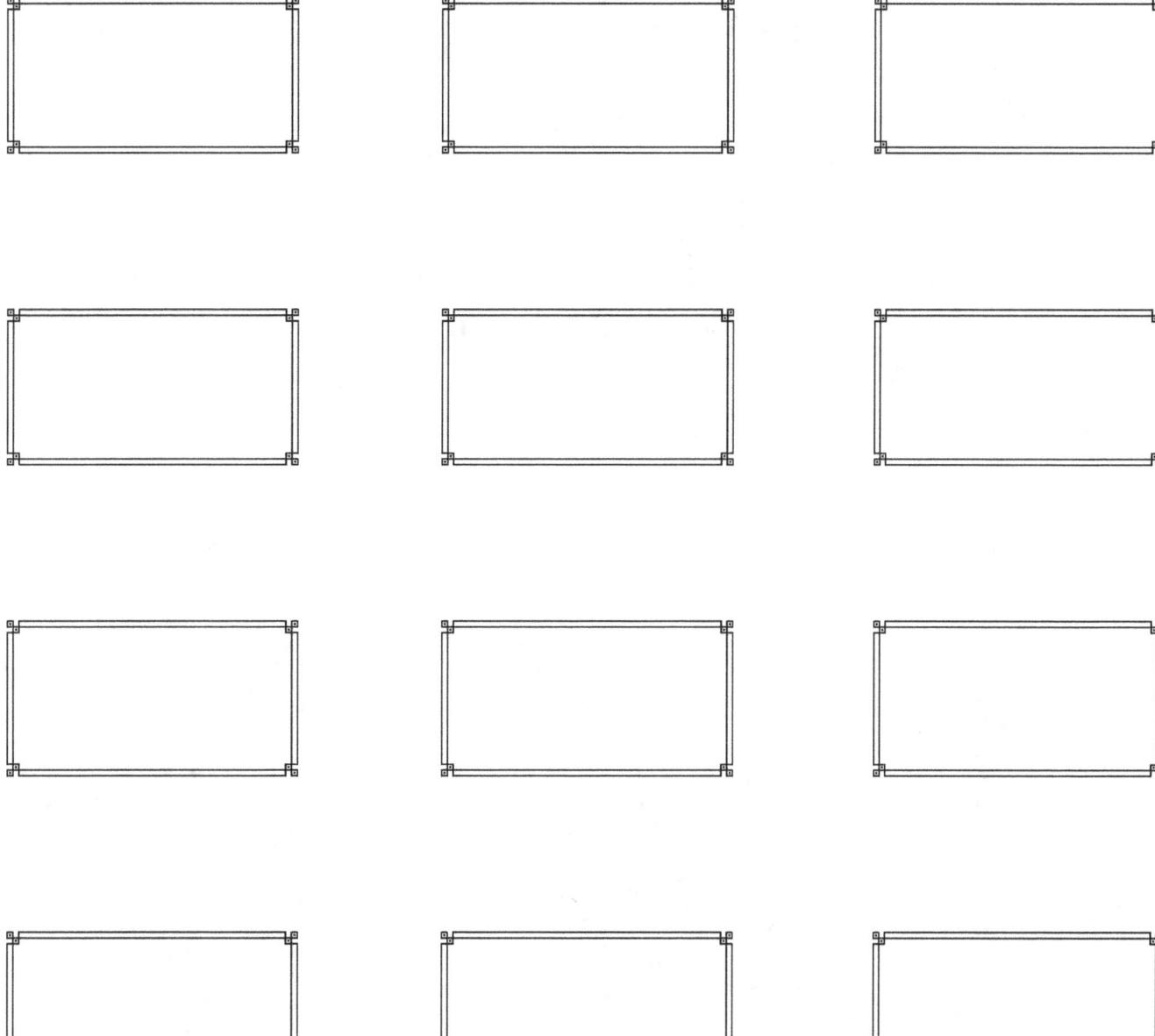

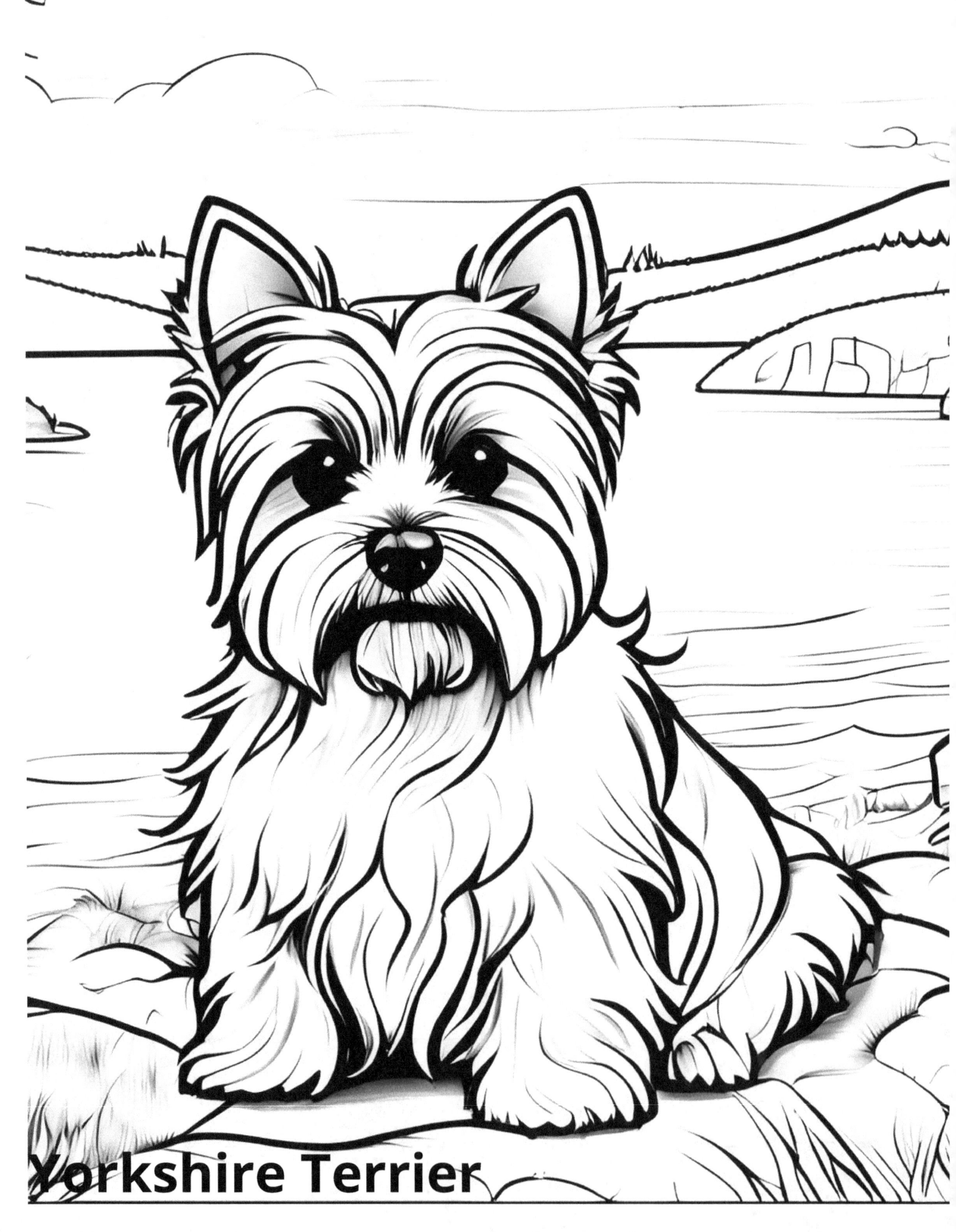

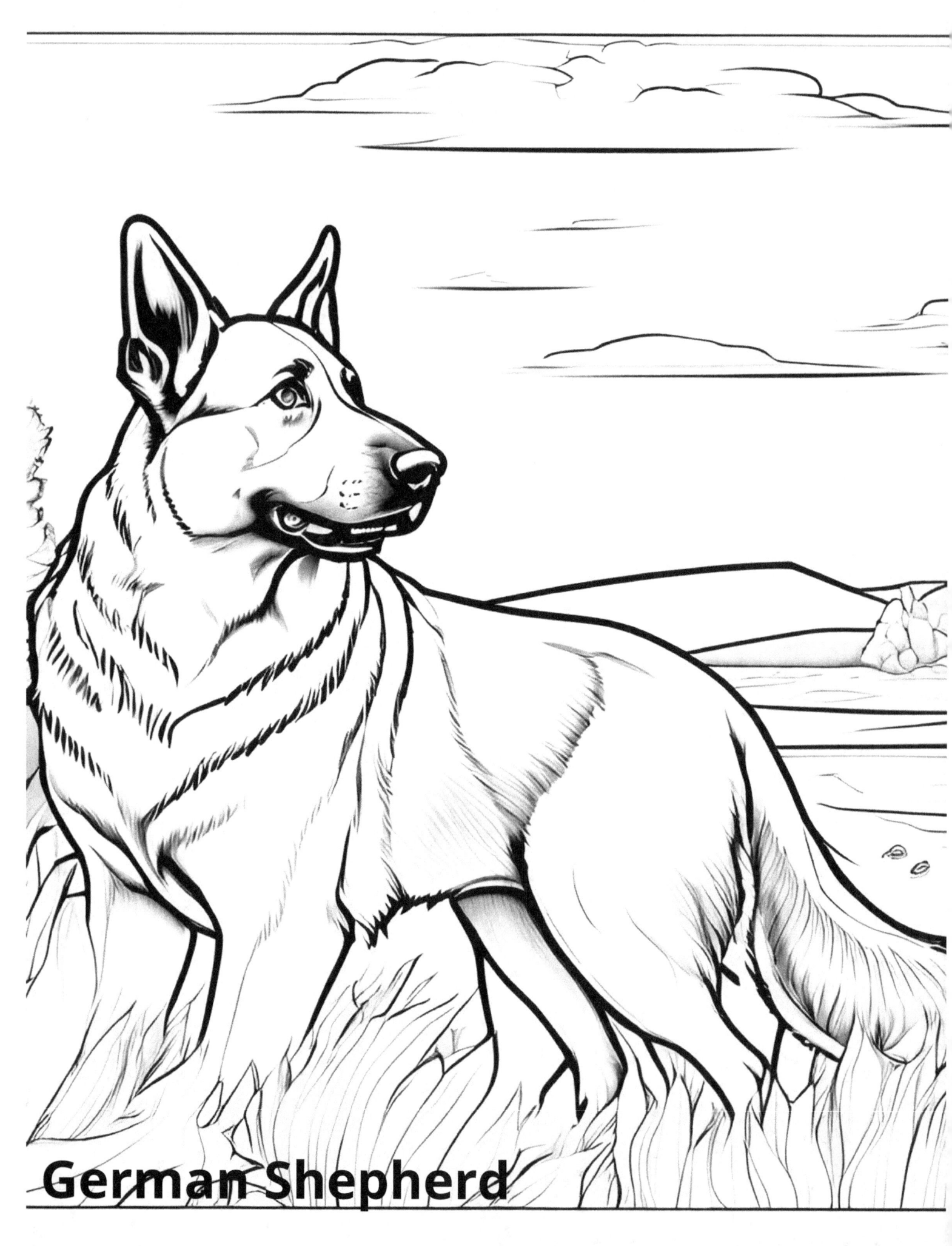

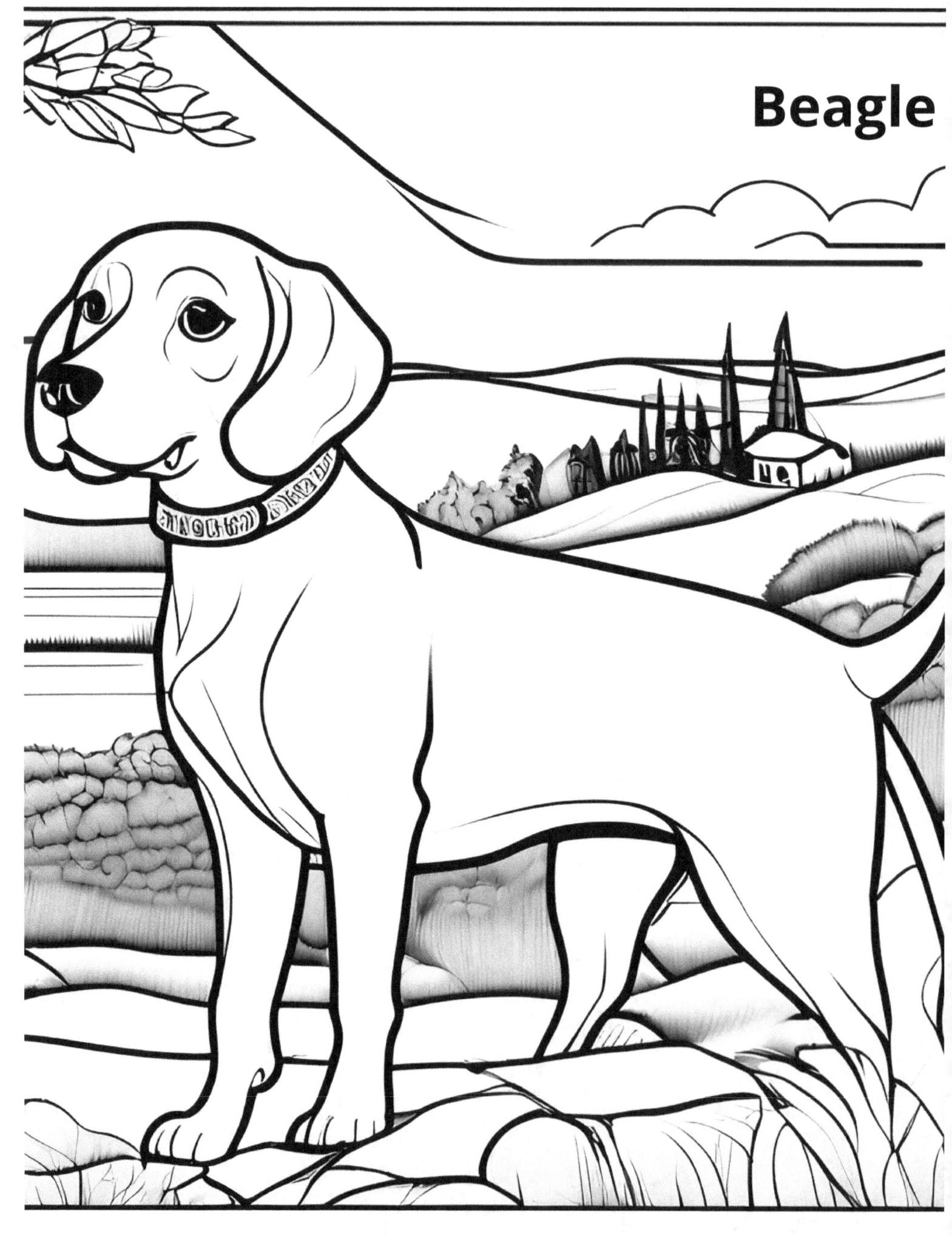

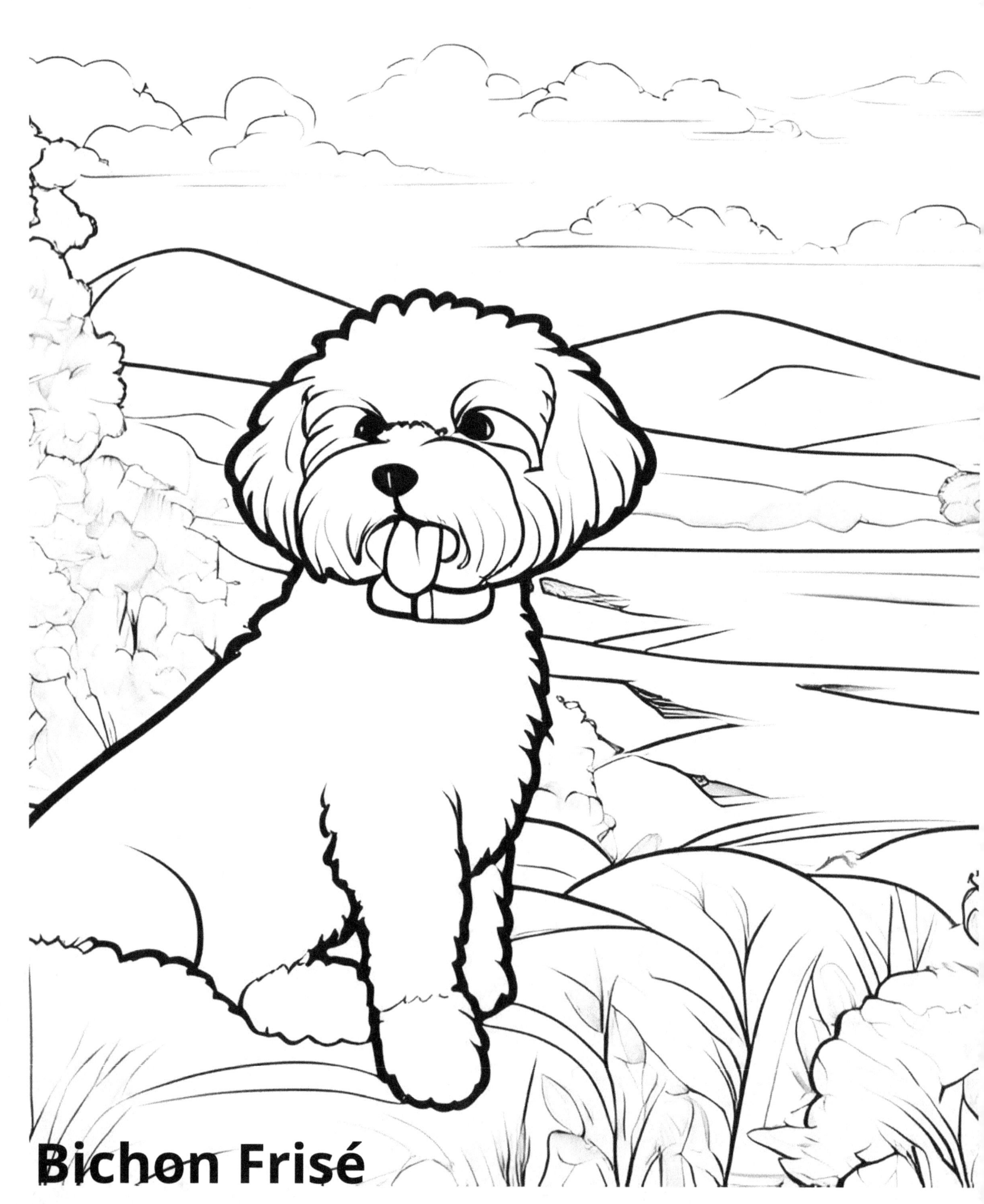

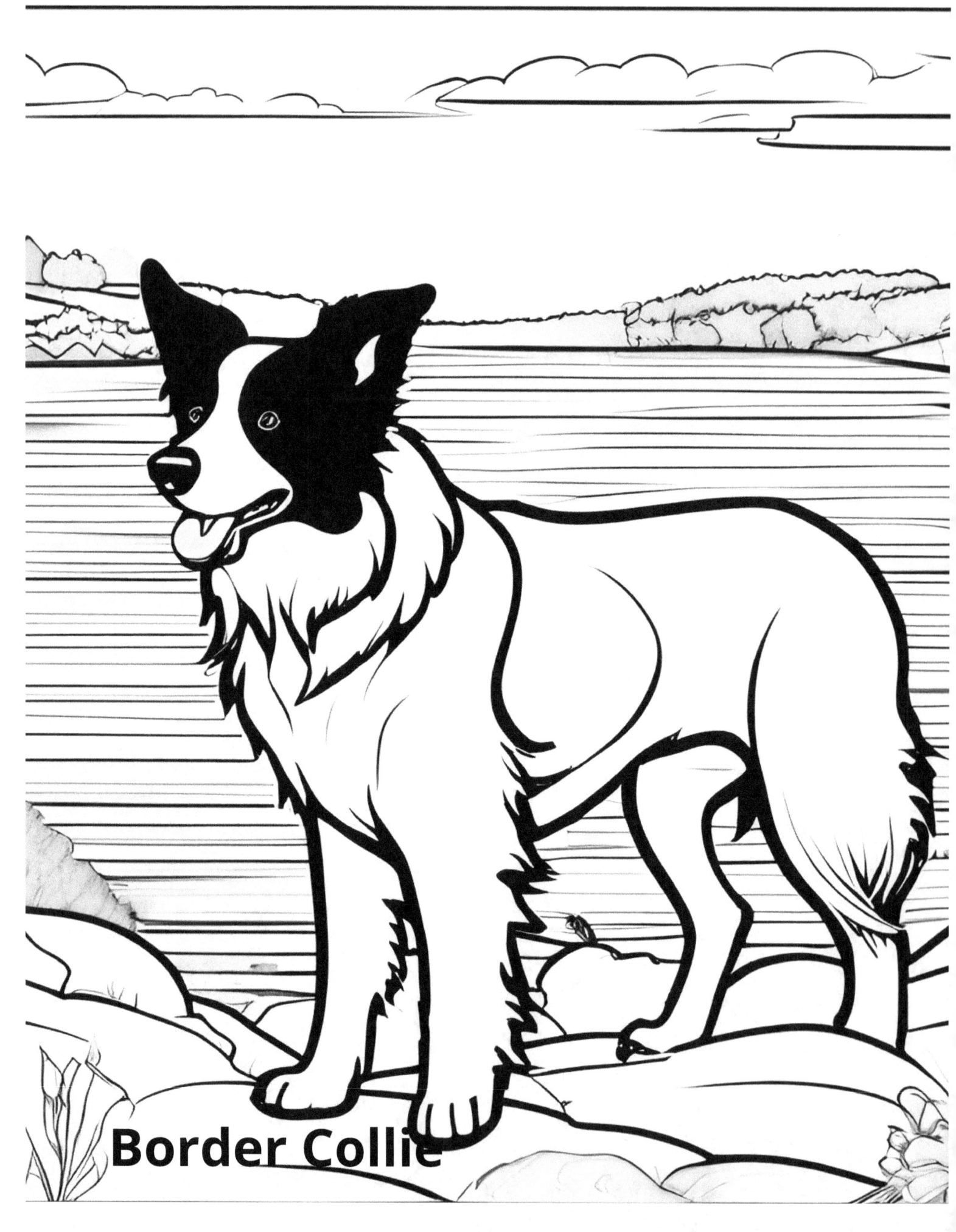

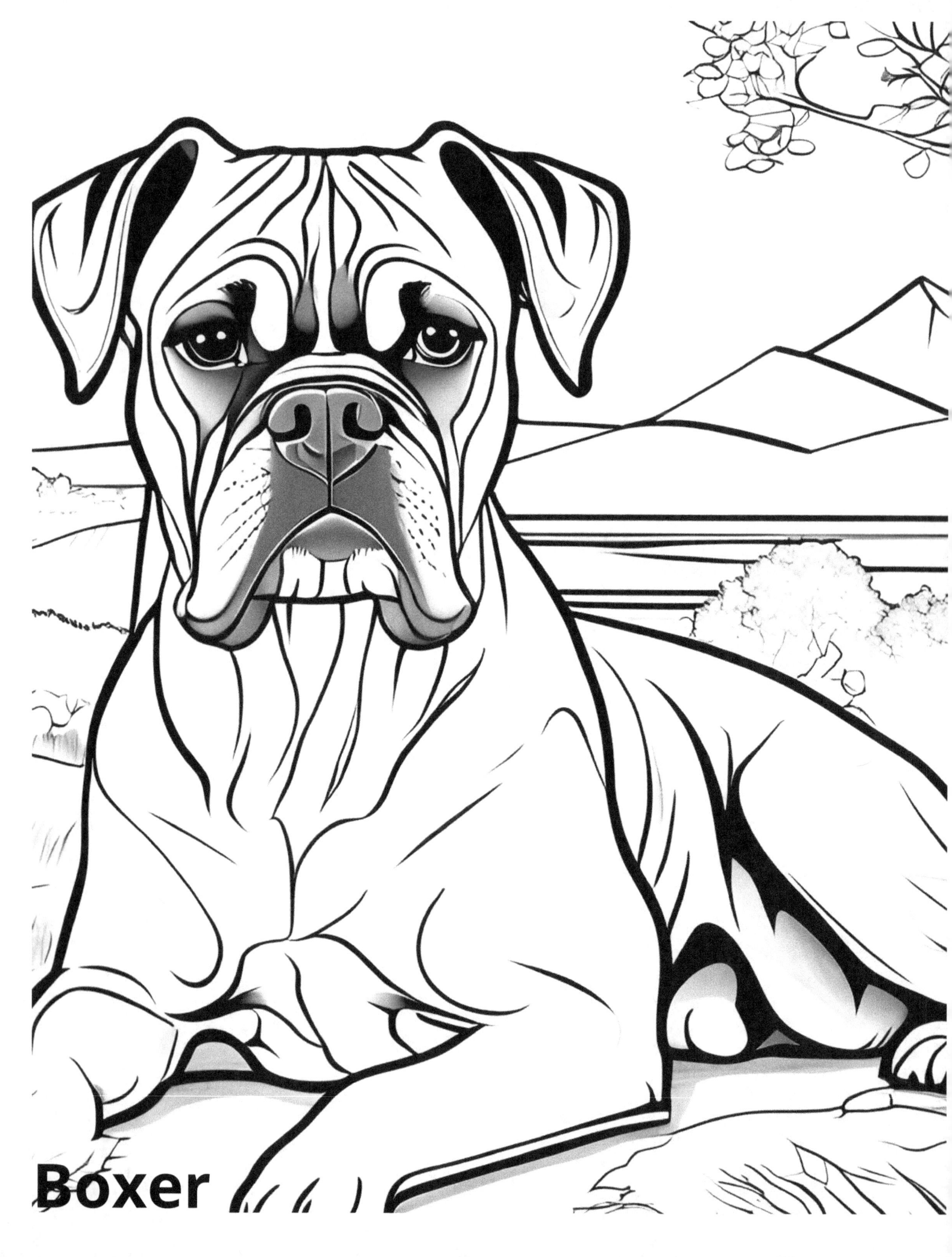

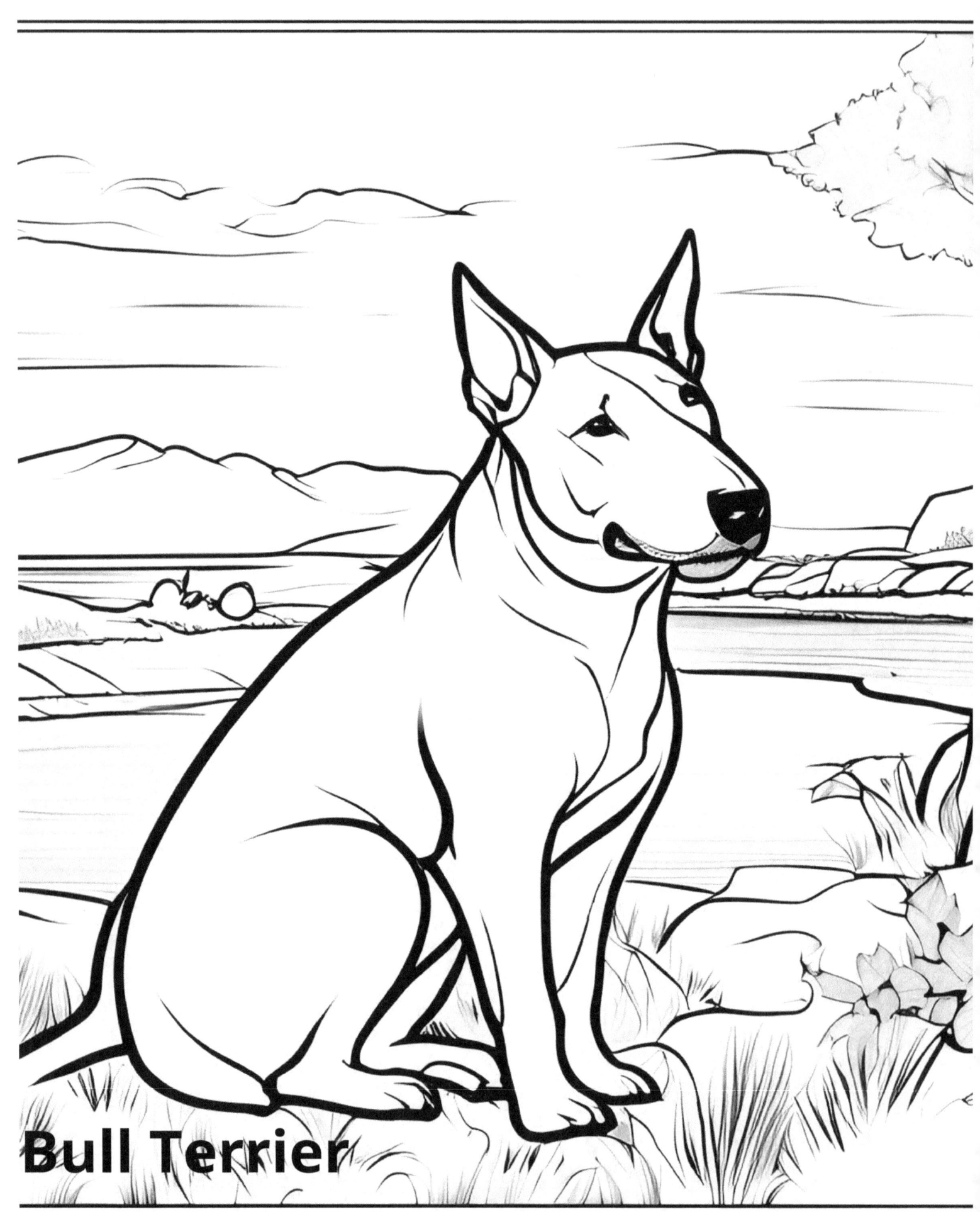

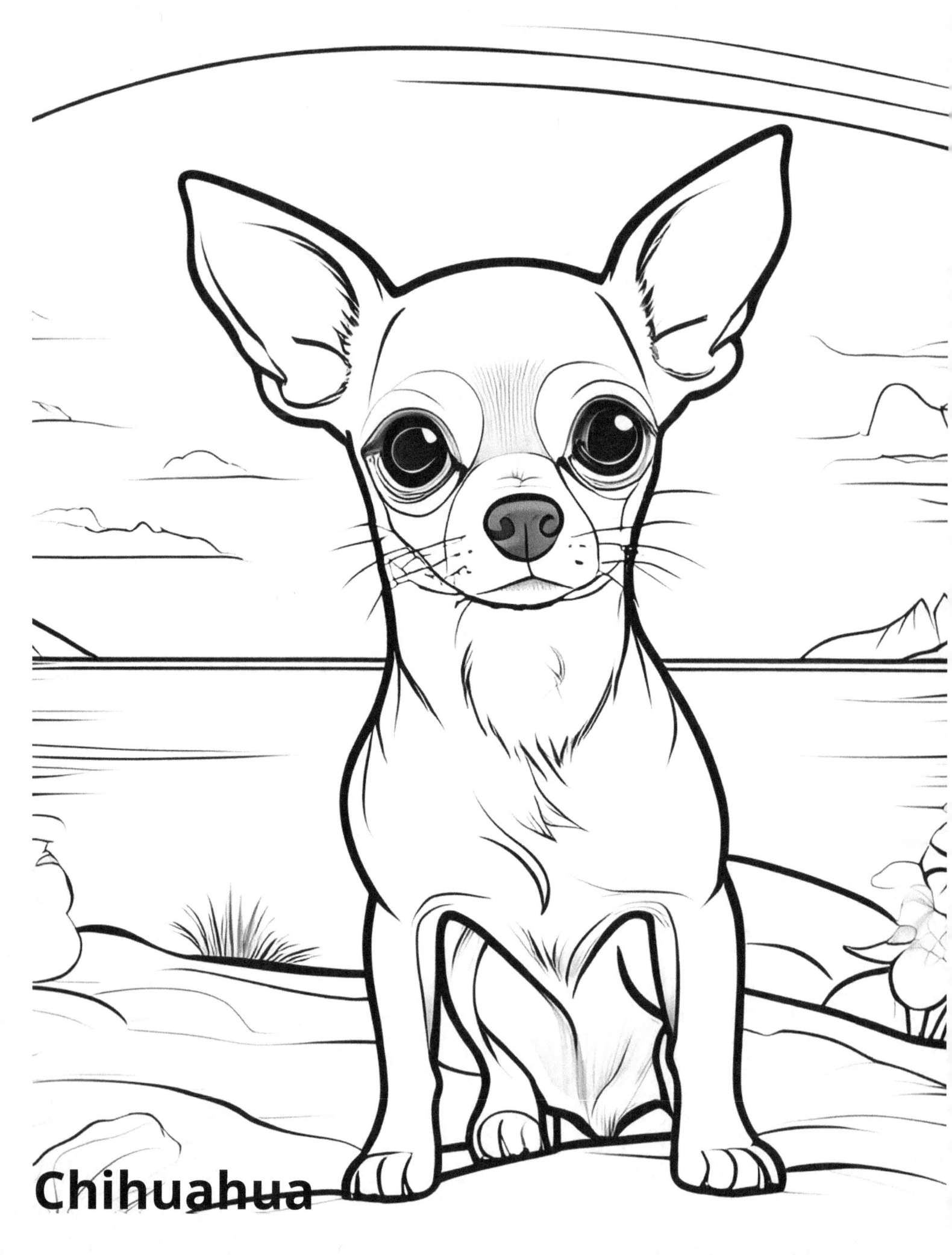

Dechshund

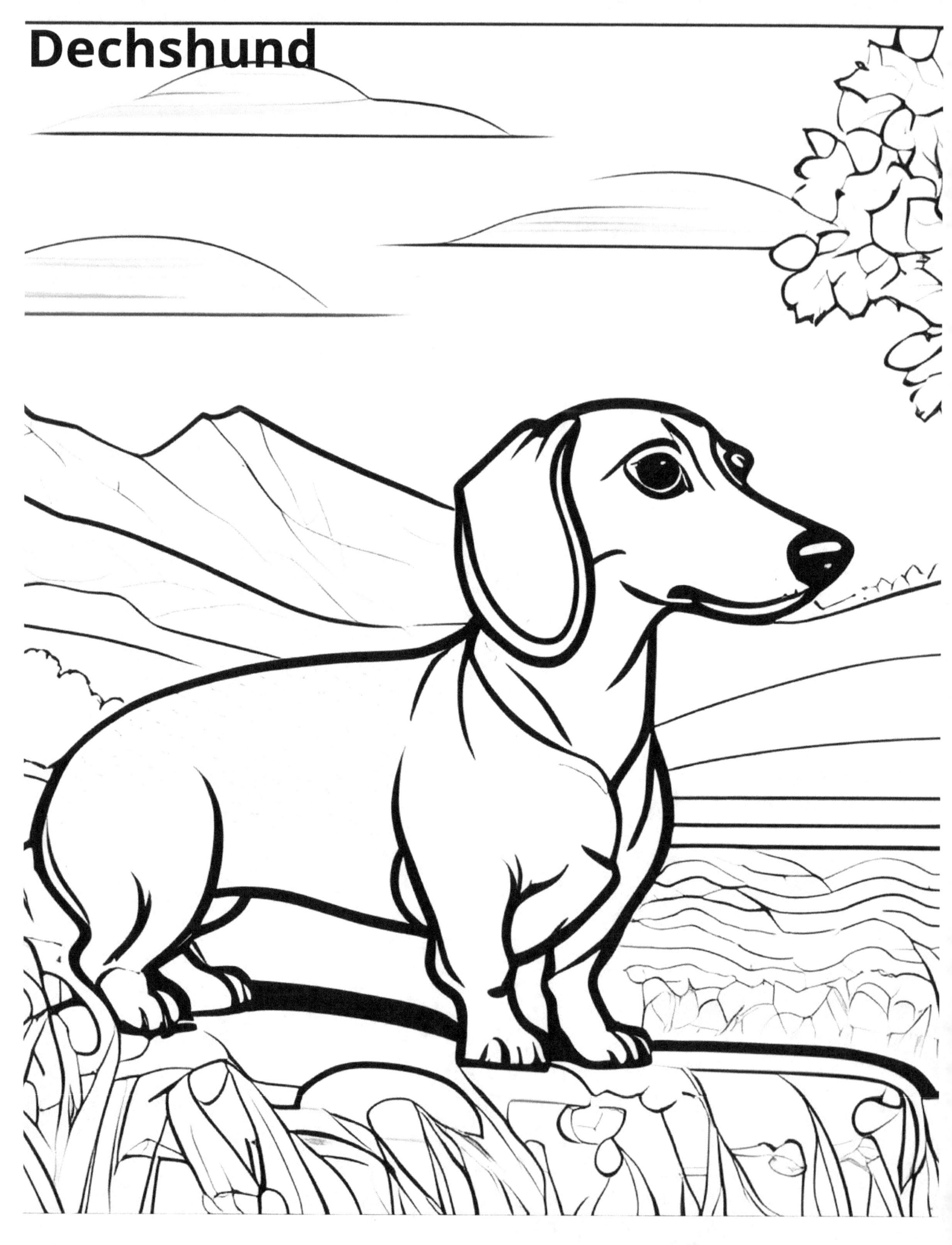

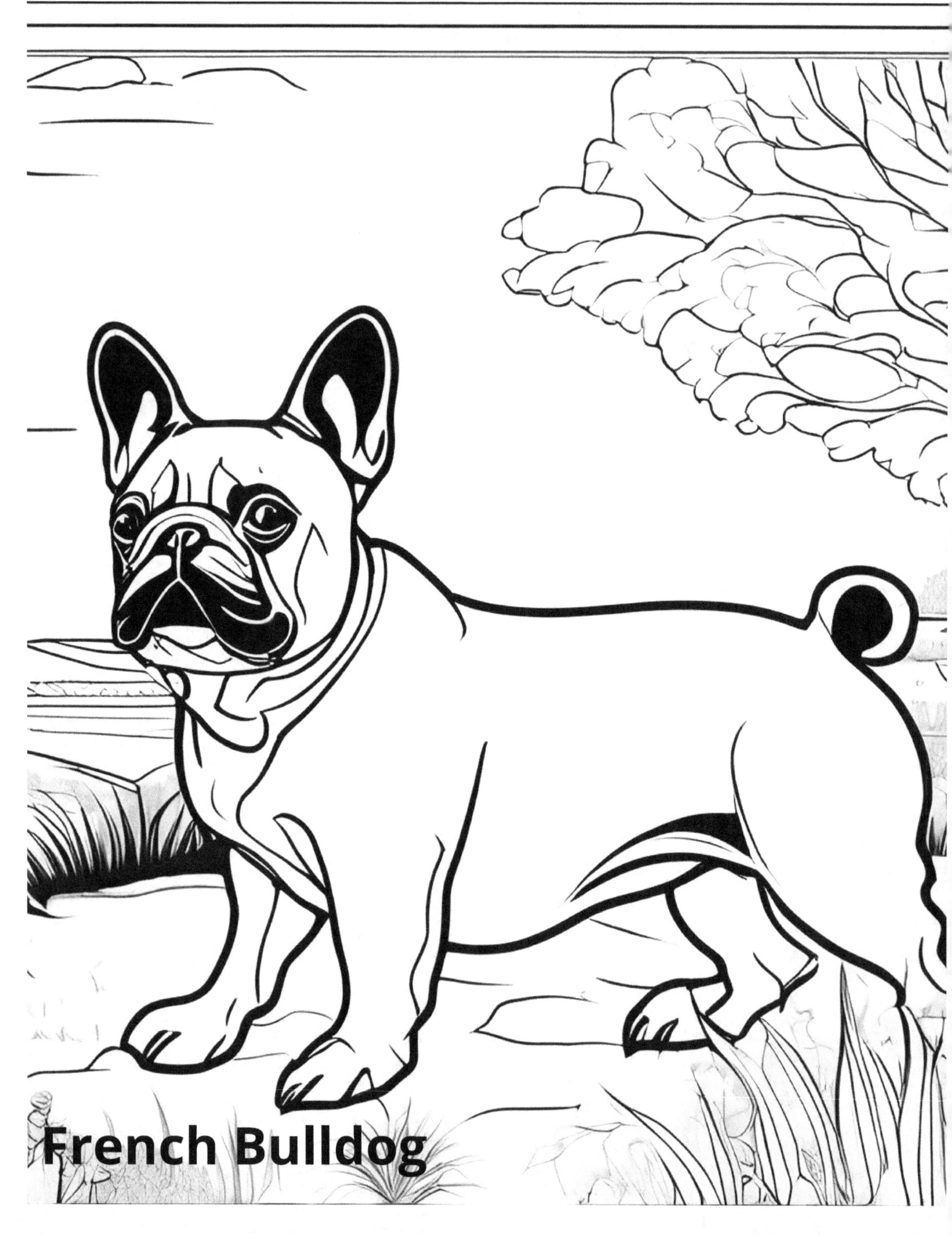

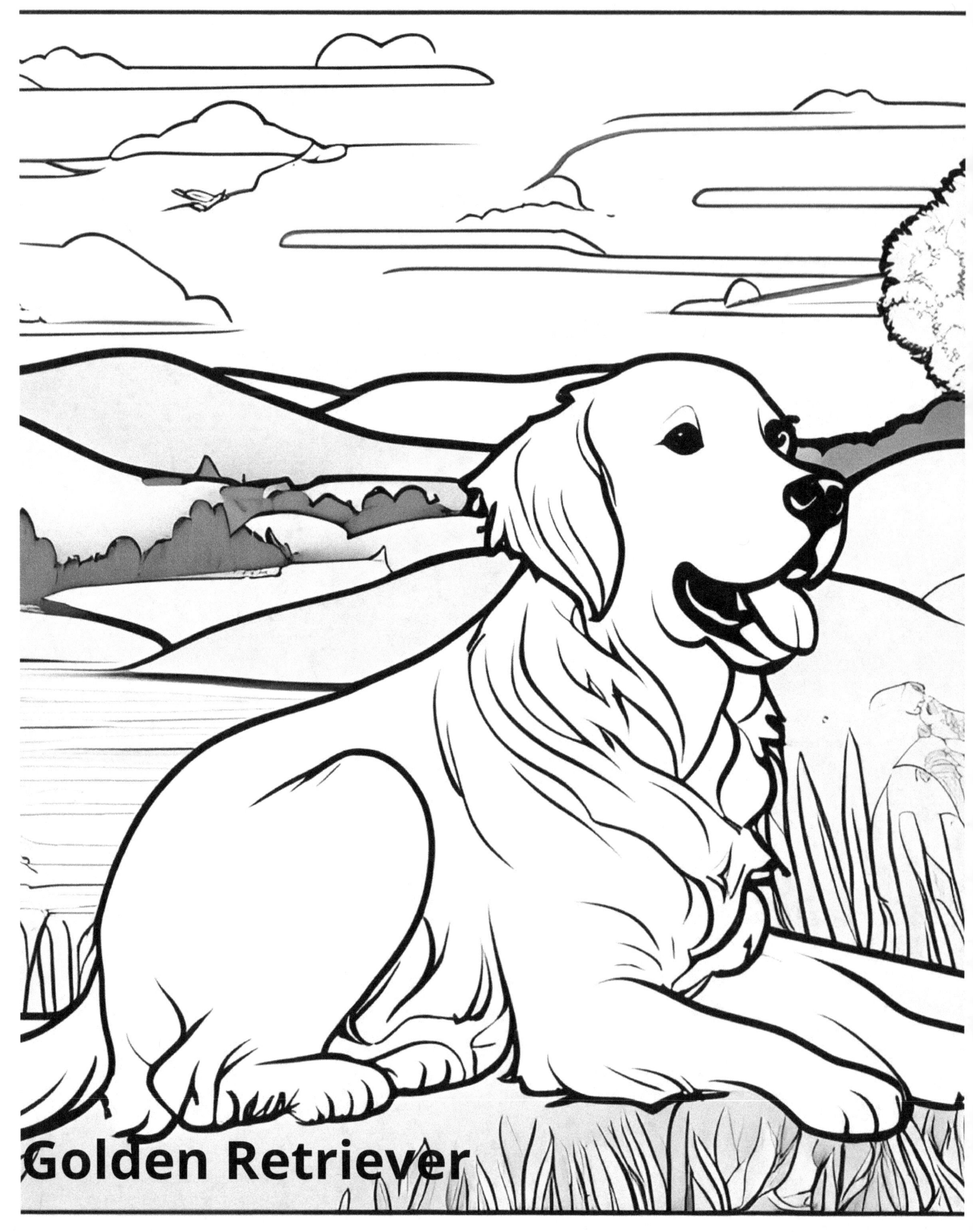

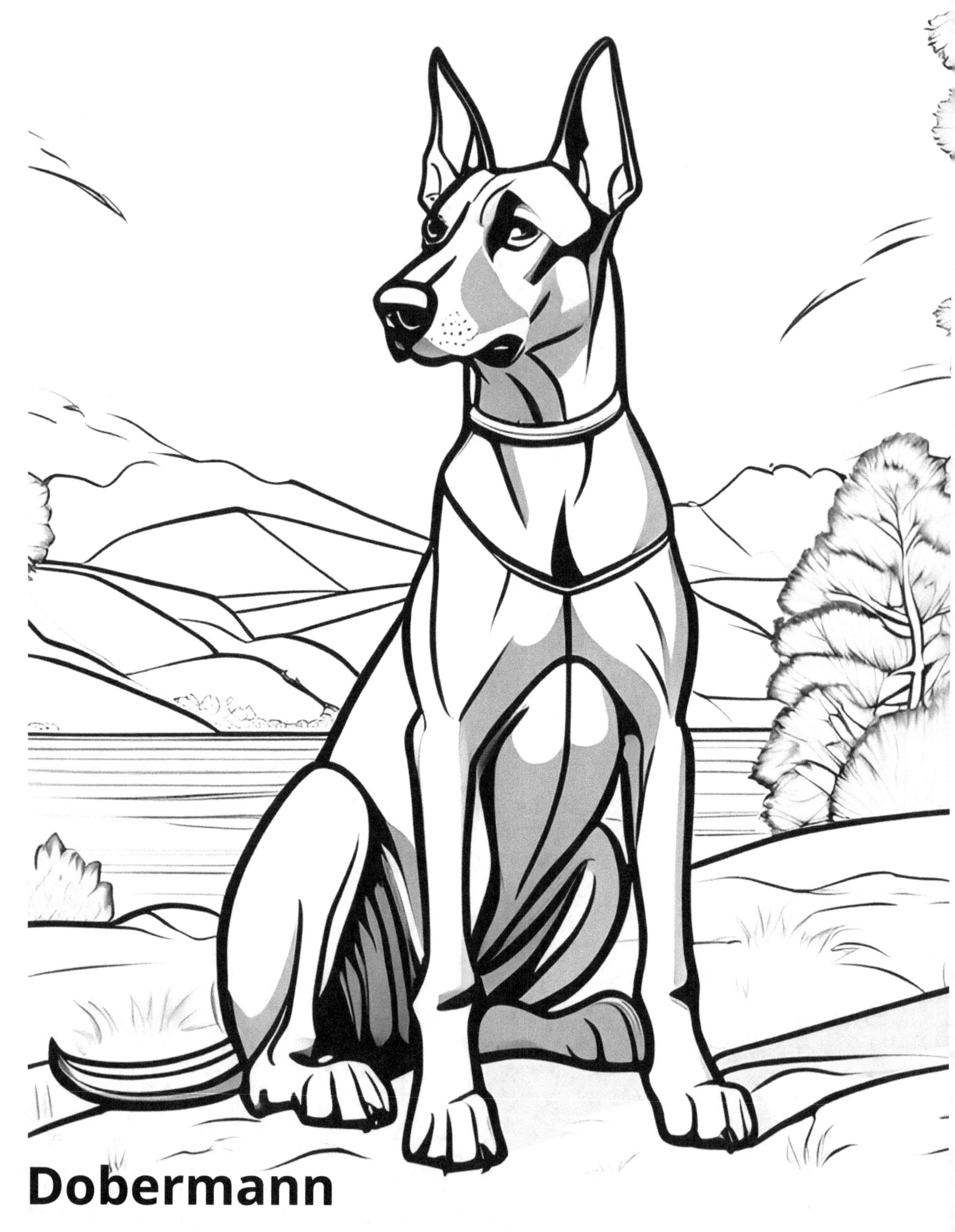

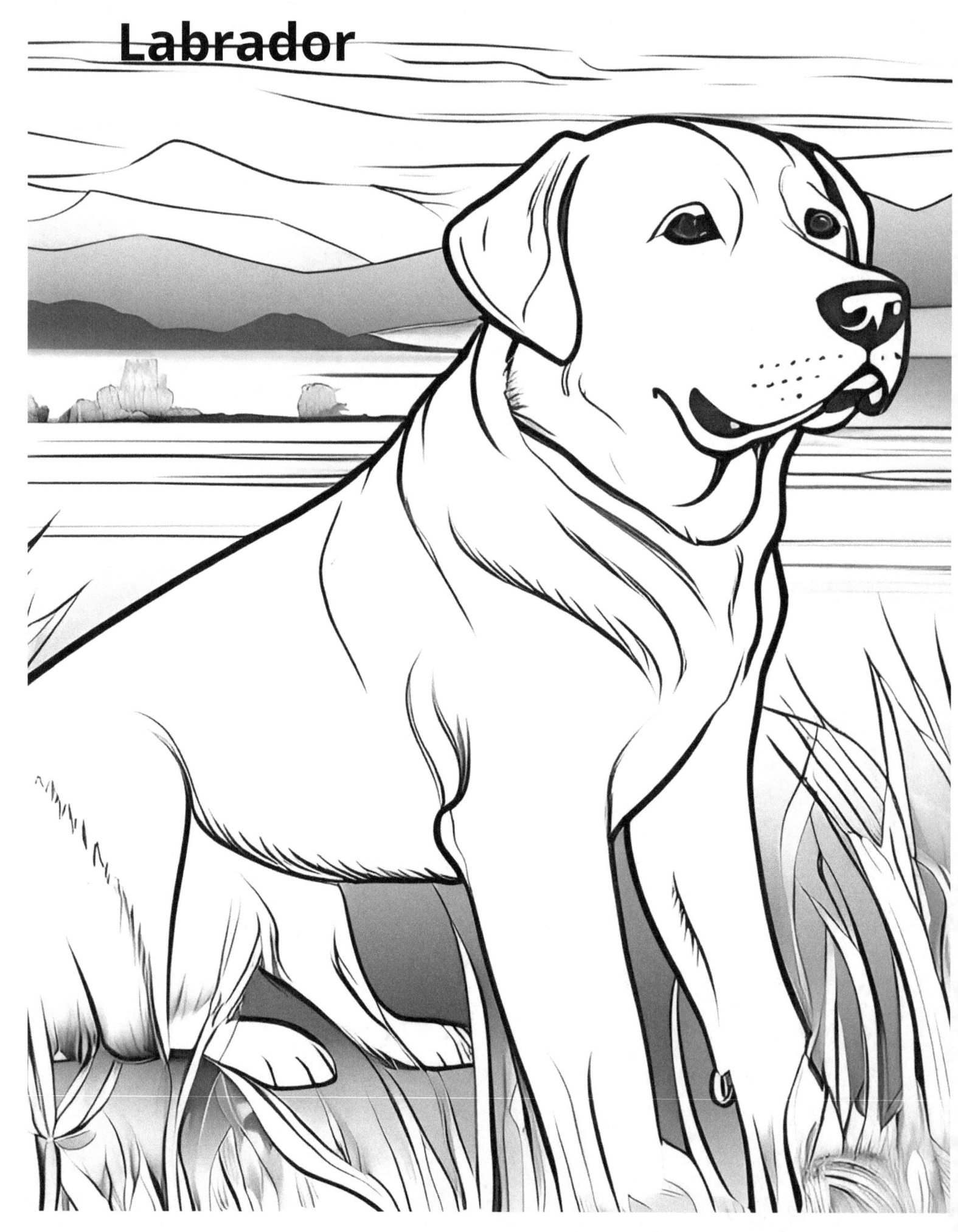

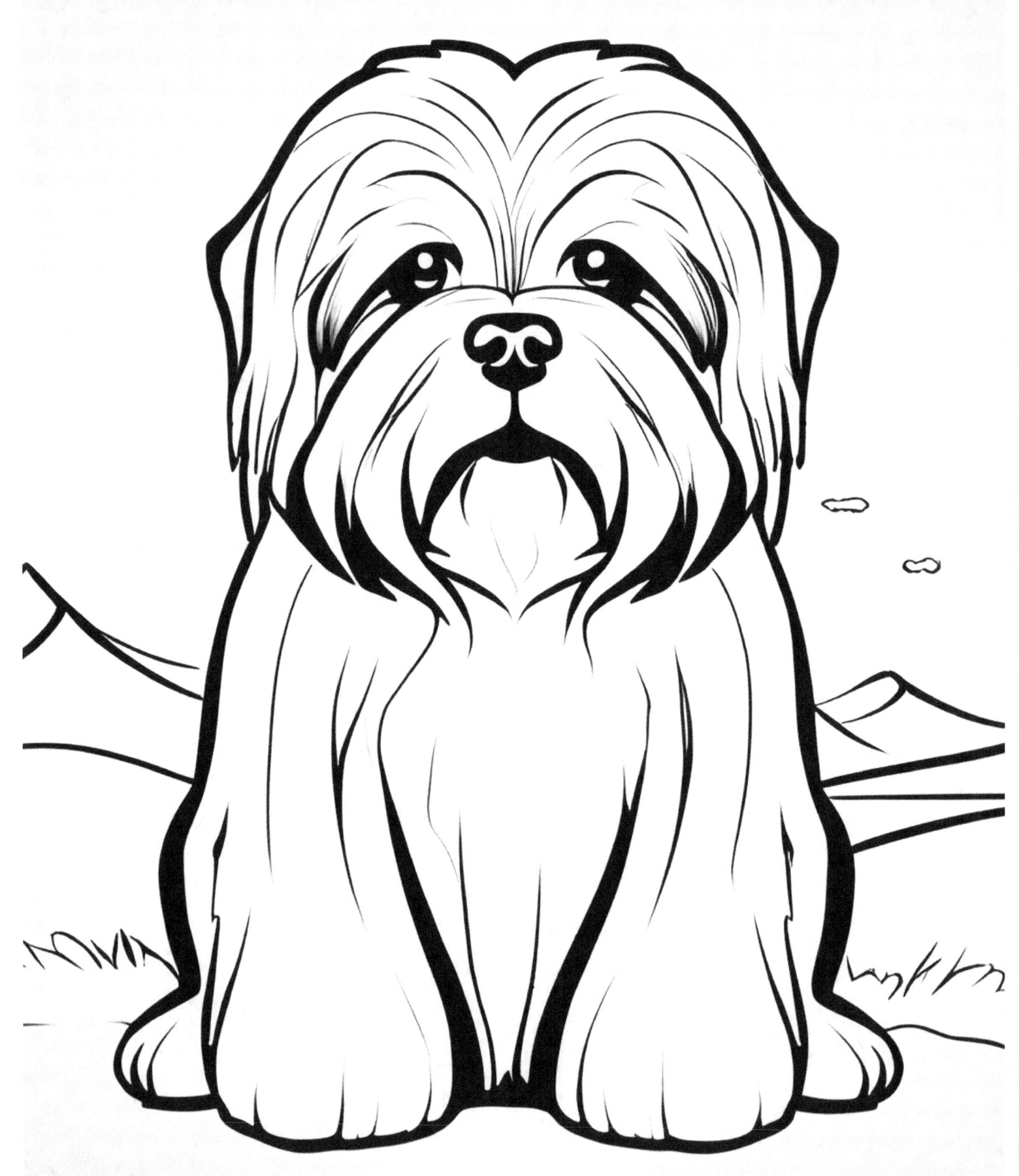

Lhasa Apso

Great Dane

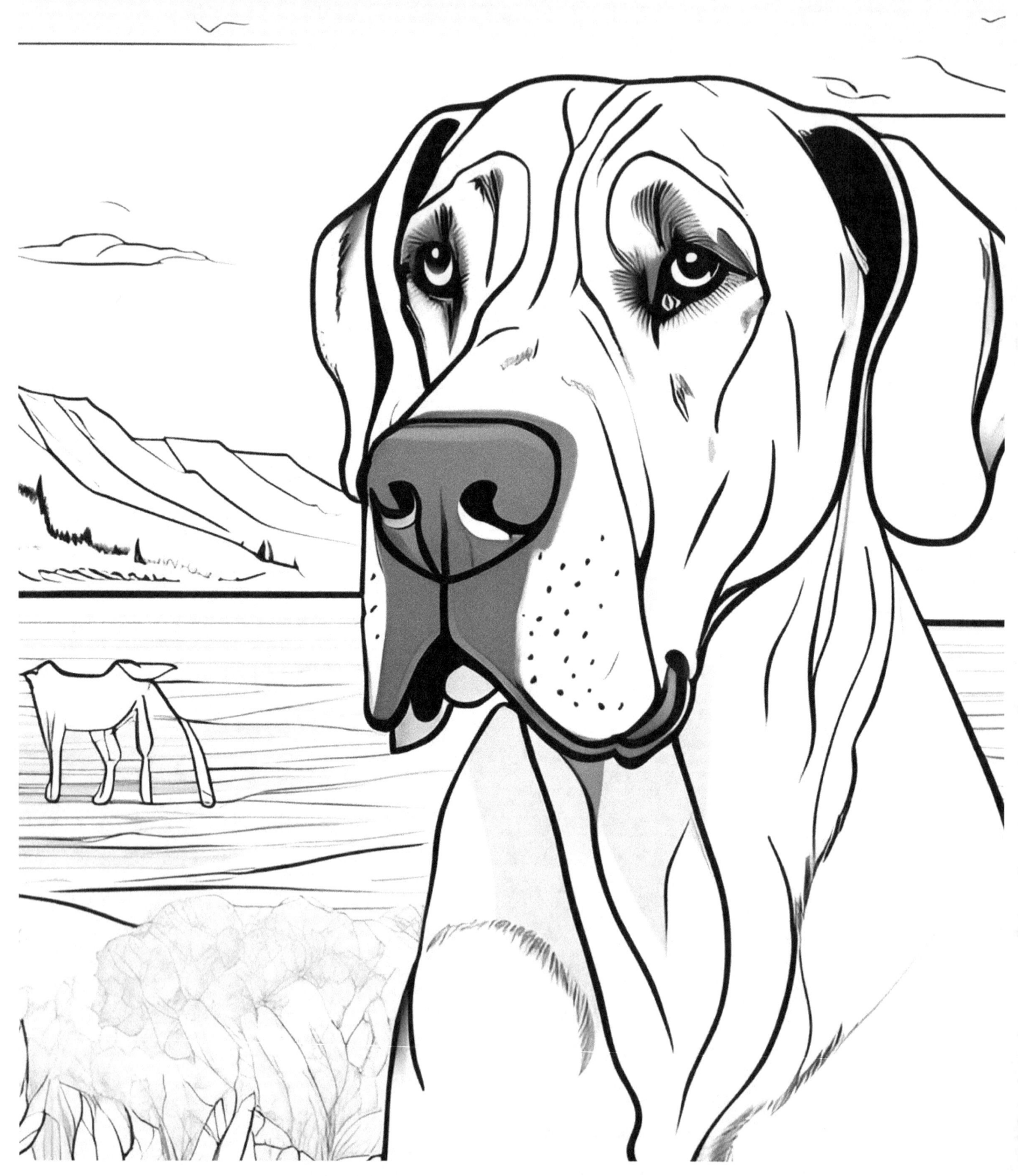

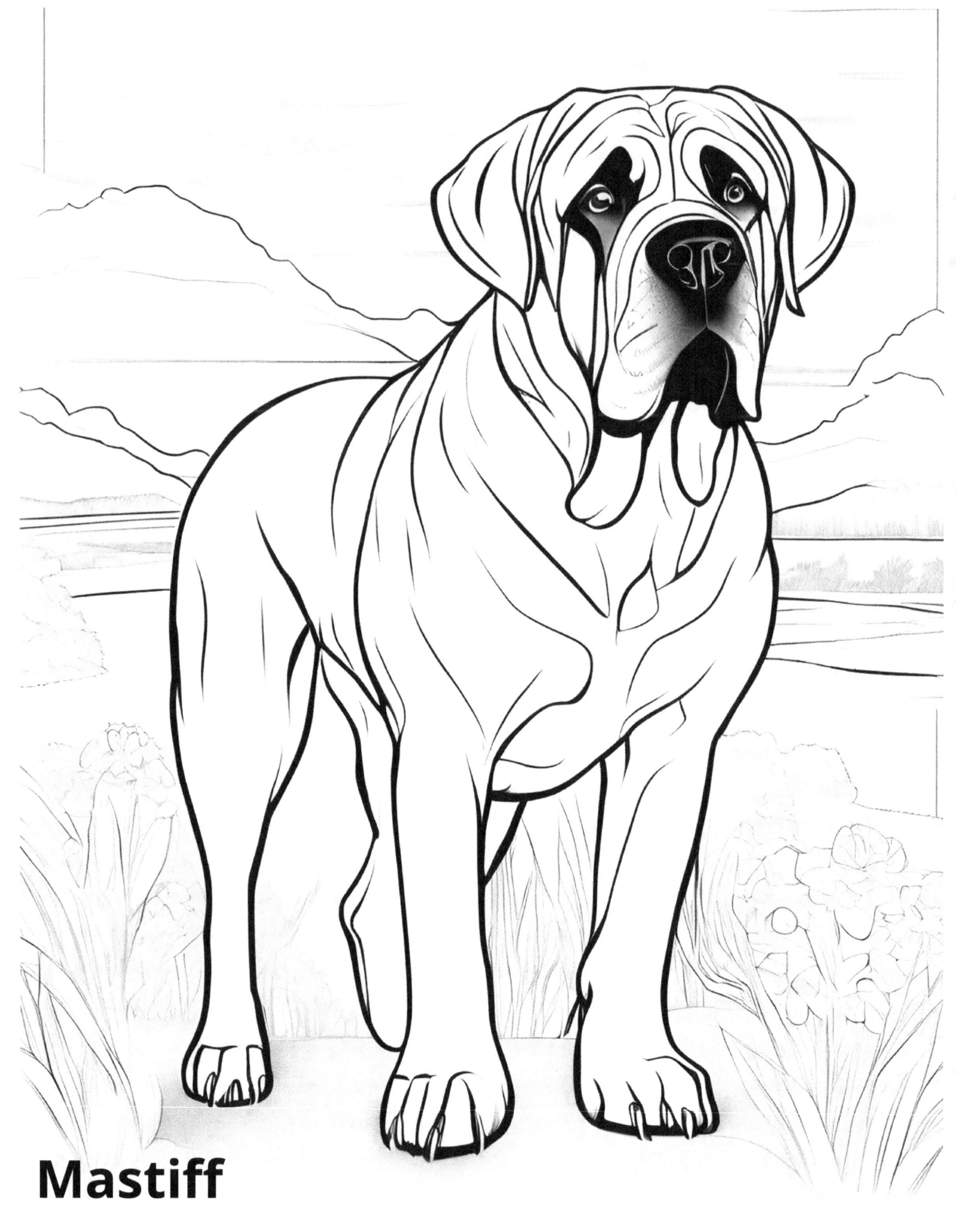

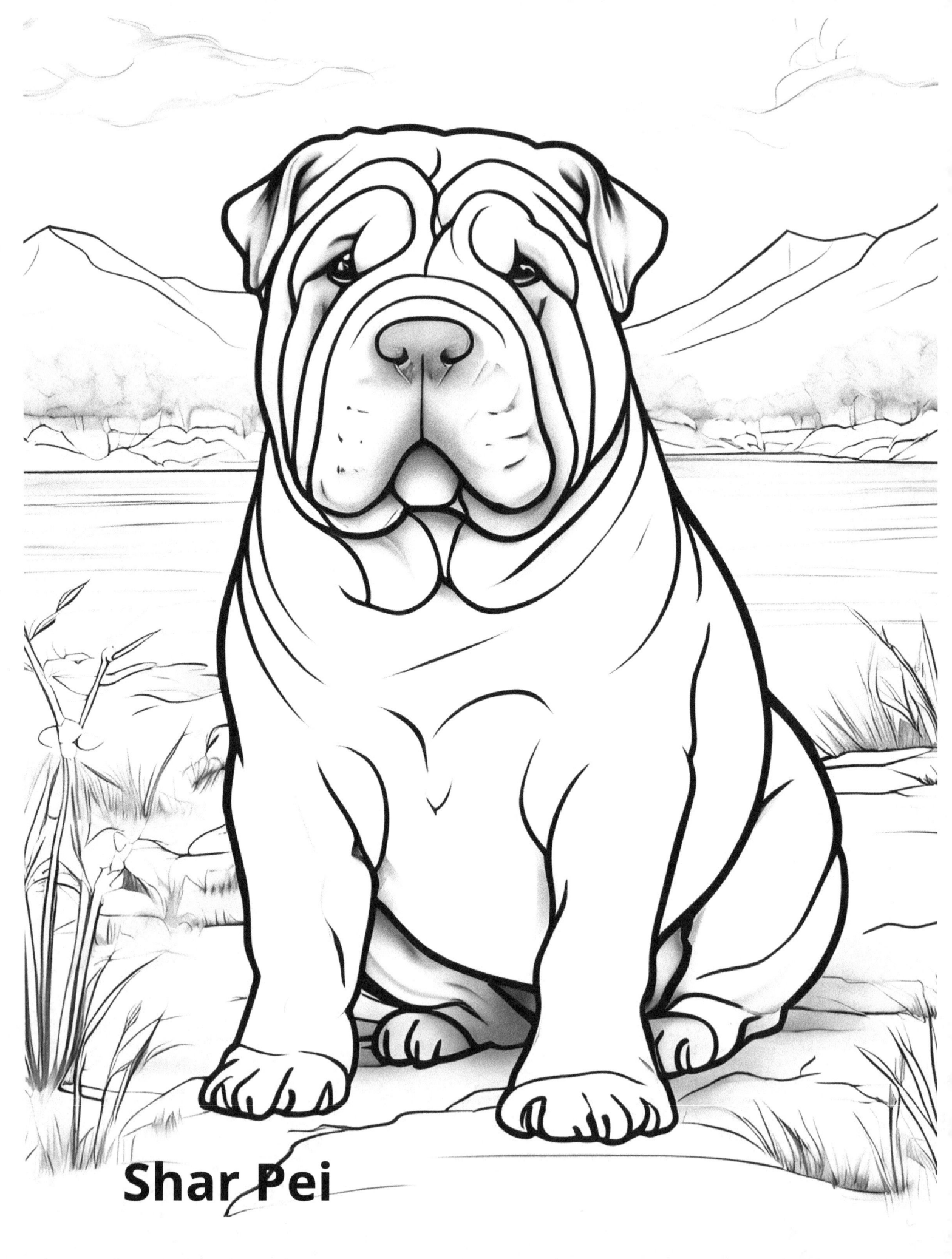

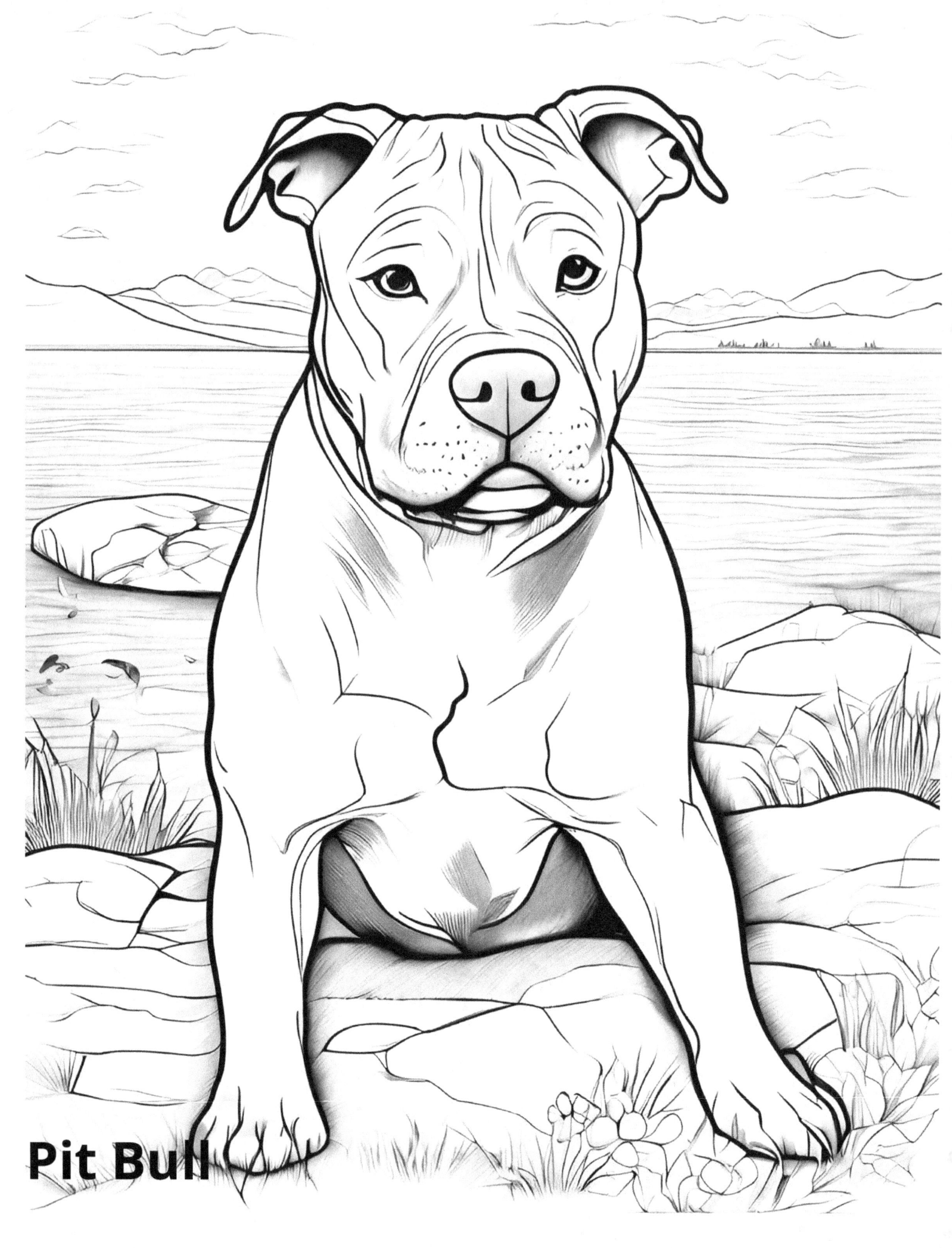

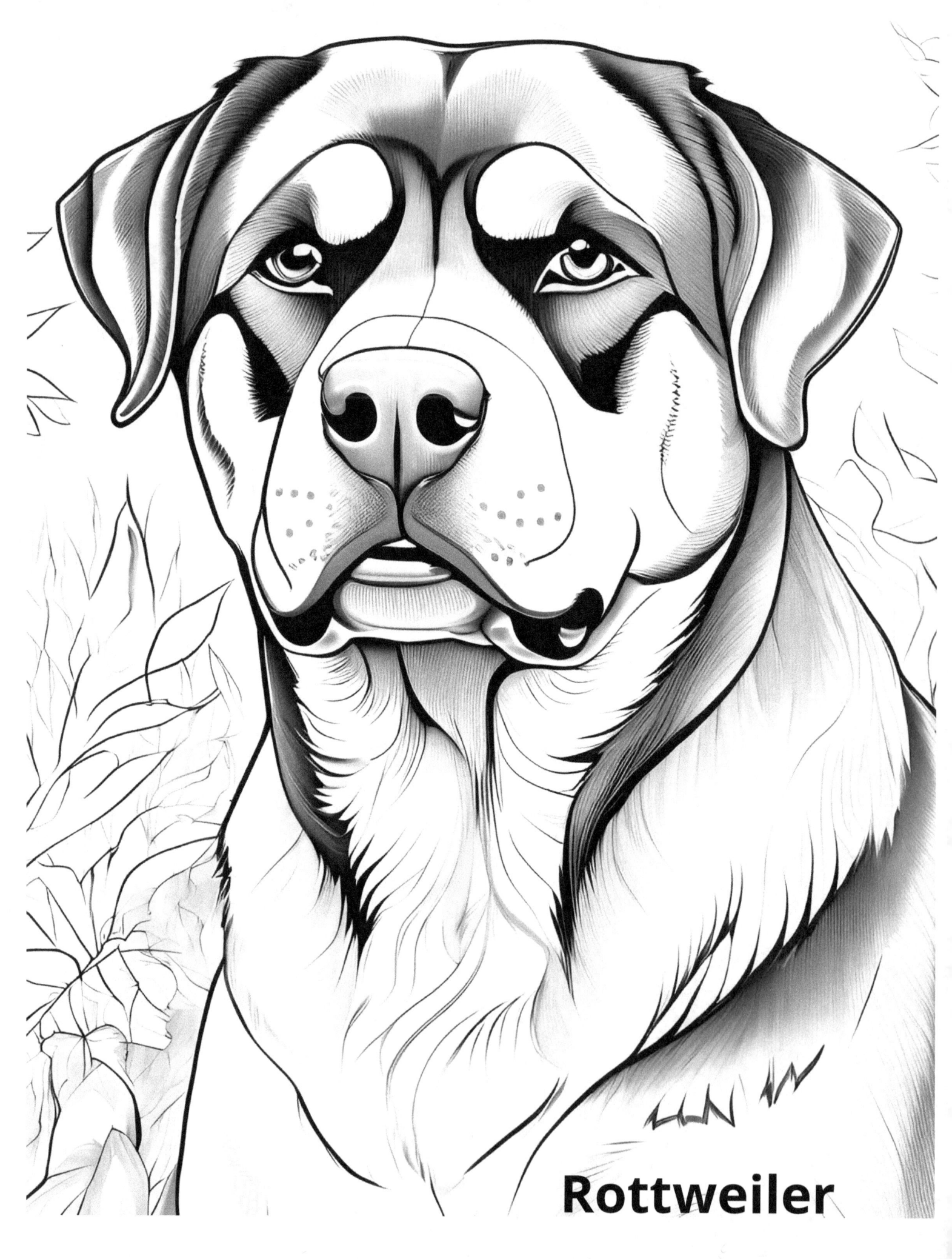

www.ingramcontent.com/pod-product-compliance
Lightning Source LLC
Chambersburg PA
CBHW081020240526
45471CB00018B/3922